Estate Planning Checklists For *Clients*

How To Get An Estate Plan That Meets
Your Needs
Not The Attorney's Needs

JULIE A. CALLIGARO

Copyright © 2016 Julie A. Calligaro

Checklist Estate Planning

All rights reserved.

ISBN: 1536914037
ISBN-13: 9781536914030

WHO WILL BENEFIT FROM READING THIS BOOK?

Most of us avoid *estate planning*, which in plain English means getting our affairs in order, until we face a life-changing event such as:

The birth or adoption of a child; the diagnosis of an illness that threatens disability or death; a family member or close friend dies unexpectedly; a new marriage with one or both spouses having children from a previous marriage. And sometimes it's just because we're about to take a trip.

I congratulate you because you've decided to take action rather than wait for a crisis or emergency. If you've made an appointment with an estate planning attorney or are about to make that appointment, this book will help you get the estate plan that meets your needs and objectives, not your attorney's needs and objectives. How do I know, because I've been an estate planning and probate attorney for 30 years.

This book does NOT include fill-in-the-blank Wills, Trusts, Powers of Attorney or Guardianship forms. If you want a do-it-yourself estate plan this is not the book for you. In 30 years as an estate planning and probate attorney, I've seen only heartache and regret from the use of do-it-yourself legal forms. It almost always turns out to be the proverbial penny-wise and pound-foolish.

My objective is to guide you, the Client, to an excellent Client experience and the estate plan that's best for you.

Best Regards!

CONTENTS

1	Who Should Prepare Your Estate Plan?	7
2	How To Prepare For Your First Meeting	9
3	What Do You Want To Accomplish?	13
4	Funding The Trust	15
5	What Should The Attorney Give You?	19
6	After You Sign The Documents	21
7	Keep Your Estate Plan Up-To-Date	23
8	Estate Planning Basics	25
9	Other Possible Estate Planning Issues	37

This Book is intended as a resource. It is sold with the understanding that the author and publisher are not engaged in rendering legal services. If legal services are required, retain an attorney. Although every precaution has been taken in the preparation of this Book, the author and publisher assume no responsibility for errors or omissions. Neither is any liability assumed for damages resulting from the use of information contained herein. The author and publisher specifically disclaim any liability, loss or risk, personal or otherwise which is incurred as a direct or indirect consequence of the use of the information contained herein.

ONE

WHO SHOULD PREPARE YOUR ESTATE PLAN?

Who Should Prepare Your Estate Plan?

I recommend that you hire an *experienced* estate planning or elder law attorney to prepare your estate plan documents. It's penny-wise and pound-foolish to do-it-yourself.

However, I also recommend that YOU control your estate planning. Tell your attorney what you want your plan to accomplish and ask what options you have including the cost of each option and the positives and negatives of each option. Then you decide (not your attorney) which option best meet your objectives.

How to Locate an Attorney

You want an estate planning or elder law attorney - an attorney who does estate planning for a living and not as a sideline. As your best source of information is a satisfied customer, ask family and friends for recommendations. Your accountant and financial planner are also good sources of recommendations.

Another source is your local Bar Association; call and ask for the names of estate planning and elder law attorneys in your area.

Cost of the Initial Consultation

Most estate planning and elder law attorneys do not charge for the initial consultation. Take advantage of the free consultation because it gives you the opportunity to judge whether you feel comfortable with the attorney and what the fees will be for the documents that you want him or her to prepare.

I'm sorry to say that some attorneys do not treat their clients well. If you are not treated respectfully by the attorney and staff; if you are kept waiting for an unreasonable amount of time; if fees are not readily and thoroughly explained; if your estate plan cannot be done in a timely manner and if your phone calls are not returned promptly, find another attorney. There are a lot of us out there.

TWO

HOW TO PREPARE FOR YOUR FIRST MEETING WITH THE ATTORNEY

How to Prepare for the First Meeting with the Attorney

You will make the best use of your time and the attorney's time if you come prepared for the meeting. Many attorneys will mail or email you a questionnaire to fill out before the first appointment. If not, here is a Checklist of the topics you should be prepared to discuss at the first meeting.

[ ] If you have an existing estate plan, bring the documents to the meeting.

[ ] Do you have a "blended family?"

[ ] Do you have a child or grandchild with special needs?

[ ] If you have minor children, who do you want to be their guardian(s)?

[ ] Do you want to avoid Probate?

[ ] Who do you want to make medical decisions for you if you cannot make medical decisions for yourself?

[ ] Who do you want to manage your finances if you become disabled?

[ ] Who do you want to be in charge of your estate at your death?

[ ] Are there charities you want to include in your estate plan?

[ ] Do you have a pet you want to make special provisions for?

Your Financial Information

To formulate a complete and accurate estate plan, you need to begin with your financial information. Here's why.

It's impossible for you and your attorney to create an effective estate plan that transfers all of your assets at your death if you don't have a complete list of the assets. It's impossible for you and your attorney to confirm that your beneficiary designations are up-to-date if you don't know who the current beneficiaries are. And it's impossible to determine if your assets are titled correctly if you're not sure whose name or names are currently on the titles.

That's why to establish an accurate and complete estate plan, you need a comprehensive list of your assets which includes the name or names currently on the title of each asset. And you need a list of your life insurance policies and your retirement plans including the names of the primary and secondary beneficiaries.

And, of course, you will need a comprehensive list of your assets to attach to your estate plan documents so your trustee, personal representative or family [maybe even your Spouse] will know what assets are in your trust or part of your estate. Discussed in further detail in Chapter 6.

What <u>Types</u> of Assets Do You Have?

To determine what your estate plan options are, the attorney will need to know the types of assets you have, and the current beneficiaries of your life insurance, IRAs and retirement accounts. Here is a Checklist of common assets:

[ ] Real state

[ ] Life insurance

[ ] IRAs

[ ] Retirement accounts

[ ] Stocks

[ ] Investment accounts

[ ] Savings bonds

[ ] Mutual funds

[ ] Annuities

[ ] Bank and/or Credit union accounts

[ ] Do you own a Business?

[ ] Asset or assets not listed above

- _____
- _____
- _____

Questions to Ask the Attorney

Here is a Checklist of Questions to ask the attorney at your first meeting. Don't be bashful, the attorney will not mind. But if the attorney is uncomfortable or unhappy with your questions, he or she may not be a good choice.

[ ] Is estate planning your primary area of practice?

[ ] How do you charge, flat fee or hourly?

[ ] If the charge is hourly, what is your best estimate of the total fee?

[ ] If I have questions will I be able to contact you personally by phone or email?

[ ] Do you return calls and emails promptly?

[ ] I want to review the documents that you prepare for me before I sign them. What is your procedure for reviewing documents and asking questions <u>before</u> I sign?

[ ] If a revocable living trust is part of my estate plan, do you prepare the documents that will transfer my assets to the trust? Is that included in the fee for the trust or is there an additional cost? **If the attorney will not prepare the documents that transfer your assets to your trust, find another attorney!**

[ ] How long will the process take from start to finish? <u>**If you are about to take a trip and want your estate plan completed before you leave, be sure you tell the attorney at your first meeting.**</u>

THREE

WHAT DO YOU WANT YOUR ESTATE PLAN TO ACCOMPLISH?

Estate Planning is not one-size-fits-all. Nevertheless, there are six objectives that are common to most Estate Plans and three additional objectives that may or may not apply to you.

The Six Most Common Estate Plan Objectives

[ ] * Name guardians for minor children.

[ ] * Name someone to make medical decisions for you if you can't make the decisions yourself.

[ ] * Name someone to manage your finances if you become incapacitated.

[ ] Avoid Probate.

[ ] At your death, transfer your assets to the person(s) you want to receive them as easily as possible. * This may include naming a trustee or personal representative.

[ ] Minimize taxes - income taxes and possibly inheritance taxes.

* When naming guardians, trustees, personal representatives and agents for financial and medical powers of attorney, always name a back-up in case the first person you've named is not able or available when you need them.

How to Avoid Probate

If avoiding Probate is one of your estate planning objectives, you have 5 ways to do so. Discuss these options with your Attorney and then choose the method that meets your objectives and is the least expensive. **Please Note that a Will Does Not Avoid Probate!**

1. Living Trust;
2. Joint Ownership;
3. Beneficiary Designations (including a Lady Bird Deed);
4. Pay on Death (POD) designations;
5. A combination of joint ownership, beneficiary designations and/or POD.

Other Possible Estate Plan Objectives

[ ] Protect governmental or other benefits that a child or grandchild with special needs currently receives or may receive in the future.

[ ] Make special provisions for a pet or pets.

[ ] Make special provisions for a charity.

Tell the Attorney what you want to accomplish and ask what options you have. Most people need medical and financial powers of attorney and guardians for minor children. But you will have choices when it comes to deciding the best method to transfer your assets at your death and to avoid Probate.

FOUR

FUNDING YOUR TRUST

"Funding" is attorney speak for changing the name or names on the titles of your assets from your name to the name of your trust. Attorneys hate funding the trust because it's time consuming and detail oriented. But for you, the Client, funding is **critical!**

Why is it critical? Because if your assets are not transferred from your name(s) to your Trust name, you have NOT avoided Probate. Case in point, a few days before writing this Chapter, I started a Probate for a family whose Mom and Dad had a trust. But the attorney who made the Trust for Mom and Dad did not change the title of their home or their cottage to the name of their Trust. Now, because Mom and Dad are both deceased, the only way to transfer the home and cottage to the Children is through a Probate.

This family will have paid twice to get the house and cottage to the Children. First Mom and Dad paid to have the Trust done many years ago. And now their Children will pay again to take these properties through Probate. The house and cottage are in different counties in the same state, which adds to the expense. But if the two pieces of real estate were in separate states i.e. Michigan and Florida, there would be Probates in both states! That's why funding your Trust is so important for you.

If Your Estate Plan Includes a Trust

So, if your Estate Plan includes a revocable living trust, your Attorney must transfer the title of your assets out of your names(s) and into the name of your Trust.

In addition, your life insurance policies, retirement accounts, IRA's, 401ks, etc. must have the correct beneficiaries and that may or may not be the name of your Trust. You must discuss this with your Attorney and make any necessary changes to your beneficiary designations.

The Trust Funding Checklist

[ ] Real estate transferred to the name of your Trust

[ ] Stocks transferred to the name of your Trust

[ ] Investment accounts transferred to the name of your Trust

[ ] Savings bonds transferred to the name of your Trust

[ ] Mutual funds transferred to the name of your Trust

[ ] Bank and/or Credit union accounts transferred to the name of your Trust

[ ] Your Business transferred to the name of your Trust

[ ] Other assets you own not listed above transferred to the name of your Trust

How to Change the Name of Your Bank and Credit Union Accounts to the Name of Your Trust

Your Attorney should prepare the documents that transfers real estate, stocks, investments, mutual funds and your business, if you have one, to the name of your Trust. However your Attorney will not be able to change the name on your bank or credit union accounts and that's for your protection. But it's essential that you change the name on your accounts to the name of your Trust otherwise there will be a Probate of these accounts at your death.

Ask your Attorney to give you the formal name of your Trust. It will be something like: " John Smith and his Successor as Trustee of the

John Smith Revocable Trust Dated July 17, 2016" or "John Smith and Mary Smith and their Successors as Trustees of The Smith Family Revocable Trust dated July 17, 2016." Then go to your bank(s) and/or credit union(s) and tell them to change the name on your accounts to the name of your Trust.

The Trust May Need to be Named the Primary or Secondary Beneficiary of Assets that Pass by Beneficiary Designation. For example:

[ ] Life insurance policies

[ ] IRAs

[ ] Retirement accounts

[ ] Annuities

And If Your Estate Plan <u>Does Not</u> Include a Trust

If a trust is not part of your estate plan, and it legitimately may not be, you must review your primary and secondary beneficiary designations on your life insurance policies, retirement accounts, IRA's, 401ks, etc. and make certain the beneficiary designations are correct. Here's an example: more often than not, I see retirement accounts with a Primary Beneficiary named but no Secondary Beneficiary. So, if you have an IRA that names your Spouse as the Primary Beneficiary but does not name a Secondary Beneficiary and your Spouse dies before you, there will have to be a Probate to get the IRA to your Children.

**Do Your Beneficiary Designations Need to be Updated?
Have You Designated Secondary Beneficiaries?**

Take this opportunity to make certain that all your beneficiary designations, both Primary and Secondary (also called Contingent Beneficiaries), are up-to-date.

[ ] Life insurance beneficiaries up-to-date

[ ] IRAs beneficiaries up-to-date

[ ] Retirement account(s) beneficiaries up-to-date

[ ] Annuities beneficiaries up-to-date

FIVE

WHAT SHOULD YOUR ATTORNEY GIVE YOU AFTER YOU SIGN YOUR ESTATE PLAN DOCUMENTS?

What Should Your Attorney Give You Before You Leave The Office?

At this point, the Attorney has prepared your Estate Plan Documents. You have reviewed the Documents and understand them. You have signed the Documents. The Attorney has also prepared the necessary funding documents which you've signed. So what should the Attorney give you before you leave the office?

[ ] Your *Original* Estate Plan Documents. The original documents are the documents with your actual signatures, which have been witnessed and notarized according to the laws of your State. Do NOT leave the original documents with the Attorney. The Attorney will keep a set of copies for his or her file.

[ ] A set of copies. You also want copies of your documents that you can keep handy and refer to easily. If the copies are lost or destroyed, it doesn't matter because your Original Documents will be in a safe place. See Chapter Six.

[ ] Copies of the Funding Documents and any Transmittal Letters.

SIX

THERE IS STILL WORK TO DO AFTER YOU SIGN YOUR ESTATE PLAN DOCUMENTS

Final Steps in the Estate Planning Process

You have a few more steps once your Estate Plan is complete. Take these steps and you will make things "as easy as possible" for those who will take over at your disability or death.

[ ] Place your Original Documents - the Trust, Will, Powers of Attorney, etc. in a safe place.

[ ] Keep the set of copies handy for periodic reviews. If they are lost or damaged it doesn't matter as you have your Original Documents in the safe place.

[ ] Inform the person(s) you've named as trustee, power of attorney, executor or personal representative where they will find the Original Documents at your disability or death.

[ ] Make certain that person can access the documents. For example, if you keep the documents in a safe deposit box, will they be able to gain access to the box? If the name of the person who will be managing your affairs is not on the box, they won't have access to your documents. If you keep your documents in a fireproof box or safe at home, make certain they know where the fireproof box or safe is and how to open it.

[ ] Shred outdated legal documents, bank and investment account statements, insurance policies, etc. You don't want to confuse the person who will be managing your affairs at your disability or death, or send them on a wild goose chase searching for an asset you sold years ago.

[ ] ATTACH AN <u>UP-TO-DATE</u> LIST OF YOUR ASSETS TO YOUR ESTATE PLAN DOCUMENTS SO YOUR TRUSTEE, PERSONAL REPRESENTATIVE OR FAMILY WILL KNOW WHAT ASSETS ARE IN YOUR TRUST OR PART OF YOUR ESTATE.

Records Stored On Your Computer

If some of your records are stored on your computer:

[ ] Make a backup of these records and put the backup in a safe place; *a place that you'll remember.*

[ ] Prepare a set of instructions for your Spouse or family so they will be able to access this information. A detailed computer file of important information is useless if your family doesn't know it exists or knows it exists but can't find it or gain access to it.

[ ] Prepare a list of your user names and passwords for on-line banking, email, frequent flier accounts, etc. Tell your family where they will find this information when they need it.

SEVEN

KEEP YOUR ESTATE PLAN UP-TO-DATE

Keep Your Family Up-To-Date

[ ] Provide information for your family about your doctors, other health personnel and your medications.

[ ] Provide information to your family about the people to contact in an emergency.

[ ] Provide information to your family about your accountant, attorney, financial advisor and insurance agent.

[ ] Provide information to your family if you have a prearranged funeral and\or burial.

Keep Your Estate Plan Up-To-Date

[ ] Review these issues yearly and at all family events that change your circumstances, i.e. marriage or remarriage, births, death, divorce, employment changes, retirement and the purchase or sale of significant assets.

- Estate Plan
- Tax issues
- Assets and debts
- Insurance policies
- Pension\retirement plans

EIGHT

ESTATE PLANNING BASICS

You are well prepared to meet with an estate planning attorney and achieve the estate plan that meets your needs and objectives. But if you want to go to that first meeting knowing about the various estate plan documents and how and when they are useful, spend a little reviewing the information in this Chapter.

How Do You Name a Guardian If You Have Minor Children?

You name a guardian or guardians for your children in a Will. The guardian is responsible for the child's day to day physical well-being. The trustee, on the other hand, is responsible for the child's money.

Who Do You Choose as Guardian?

The following information will help you select a guardian for your minor children. It's sensible to talk to the person(s) you have in mind to make certain they are willing to act as your children's guardian <u>before</u> your attorney prepares the documents.

Most parents strive to name a guardian who shares their values. Elements to consider include the proposed guardian's religious background, lifestyle and living situation.

Since the financial responsibility will rest with the trustee, the guardian's financial qualifications are of lesser importance. Nevertheless your child will certainly be influenced by the guardian's behavior so choosing a person who is financially responsible is important. However, if the person named as guardian is also qualified to manage the child's money, the guardian can also be the trustee.

Although nothing prohibits you from appointing someone who resides in another state, take residency into consideration especially if the proposed guardian lives far away from other close family members.

An Individual vs. a Couple

Parents often name a married couple to be guardians. But consider who would remain the guardian in the event the couple divorces or one member of the couple dies. When pressed on this issue, "my sister and brother-in-law" is really "my sister." In the event of your sister's death, do you want your brother-in-law or someone else to be the guardian? Your Will should reflect your true preference by naming only the desired individual or individuals. Nevertheless if a couple is appropriate name them.

A Sibling

You can name an adult child to act as the guardian for your younger children. Although this may help maintain family stability, it's a substantial responsibility for the older child. In addition to the enormous change moving from the role of older sibling to the role of stand-in parent, the responsibility associated with acting as guardian may put too much pressure on the siblings' relationship. In seeking the best solution for the younger children, this plan has the potential to cause unintended harm to your older child.

Who Will Manage Your Finances if You Become Incapacitated?

You have two ways to name someone (a spouse, child, family member of friend) to manage your finances if you become incapacitated: a financial power of attorney and a living trust.

Financial Power of Attorney

A financial power of attorney is a legal document that names someone you TRUST as your "agent" should you become incapacitated. You may need this person to pay your bills, do your banking, file your tax returns, collect rents, etc.

A power of attorney takes effect <u>either</u> at the time you sign the document <u>or</u> at the time you become incapacitated. It's more convenient for you and your family if the Power of Attorney takes effect when you sign it. Here's why, before a Power of Attorney can take effect when you've become incapacitated, you must be examined by a doctor who must certify in writing that you are unable to manage your affairs. Be sure to discuss these options with your attorney.

Four Important Points About Financial Powers of Attorney:

1. You cannot sign a Power of Attorney if you are incompetent, so advance planning is essential.

2. A Power of Attorney gives the person you've selected control over your finances so you must choose a person you **trust.**

3. Name an alternate in case the first person you've named is not available or able to act as your agent.

4. A Power of Attorney terminates at your death.

Living Trust

A living trust is an alternative to a financial power of attorney. If you have a trust and then become incapacitated, your successor trustee takes over the management of the trust assets (your finances) during your disability or incapacity.

Who Will Make Medical Decisions for You if You Cannot Make Them for Yourself?

Medical Power of Attorney

A medical power of attorney is a legal document that names someone you TRUST to make medical decisions for you if you cannot make the decisions yourself. You can appoint your spouse, child, family member or friend. A medical power of attorney is also known as a health care proxy and a patient advocate designation.

Three Important Points About Medical Powers of Attorney:

1. You cannot sign a Power of Attorney if you are incompetent, so advance planning is essential.

2. A Power of Attorney gives the person you've selected the authority to make your medical decisions, so you must choose a person you **trust**.

3. Name an alternate in case the first person you've named is not available or able to act as your agent.

I strongly recommend that you have a face to face discussion about end of life decisions with the people you select to make medical decisions for you. If your spouse or children have to make a "turn off the machine" decision, it will be easier for them if you've discussed how you feel and what you want and expect them to do.

Living Will

A living will is a document that expresses your wishes concerning the use of artificial or life-support measures if there is no reasonable expectation you will recover. A Living Will can be a separate document or incorporated into a Medical Power of Attorney.

How Will You Transfer Your Assets at Your Death?

You have options:

1. Beneficiary Designation;

2. Joint Ownership;

3. Will;

4. No Will;

5. Living Trust.

1. Beneficiary Designation

Certain types of assets allow you to name a beneficiary who will receive the asset at your death. Examples of assets that allow you to name a beneficiary are: life insurance policies, annuities, IRAs, and certain types of bank and brokerage accounts. Bank and brokerage accounts that allow you to name a beneficiary or beneficiaries are called "Transfer on Death" (TOD) or "Pay on Death" (POD).

Assets that pass by beneficiary designation go directly to the beneficiary you have designated thereby avoiding Probate. However, if your beneficiary dies before you and you have not named a secondary (also called contingent) beneficiary the asset must go through Probate.

Lady Bird Deed

Think of a Lady Bird Deed as a beneficiary designation for real estate. You can designate a "beneficiary" for your real estate thereby avoiding Probate. Once again if your beneficiary dies before you, the asset must go through Probate.

This is how a Lady Bird Deed works. At your death the Lady Bird Deed conveys the real estate to the person or persons whose name or names are on the deed. However, as long as you are alive, you can change the deed WITHOUT the cooperation of the person or persons you've previously named.

For example, your attorney prepares a Lady Bird Deed which conveys your house to your son at your death. If you don't change your mind, the property will belong to your son at your death.

But if you do change your mind and decide to give the house to your daughter instead of your son, you can have a new Lady Bird Deed prepared which now gives the house to your daughter.

The appeal of a Lady Bird Deed is that you remain in control of your property for as long as you live. You will see how a Lady Bird Deed differs from Joint Ownership when you read the next section.

2. Joint Ownership

If the title of an asset is in your name and the name of another person(s) as "joint tenants with rights of survivorship," the asset passes directly to your joint tenant at your death thereby avoiding Probate. Examples of assets that you can own as joint tenants are real estate, bank and brokerage accounts, savings bonds and stock certificates.

However, if your joint tenant dies before you die, the asset will then be in your name alone. And unless you name a new joint tenant, the asset must go through Probate at your death.

There are <u>disadvantages and risks</u> in owning an asset as a joint tenant with someone other than your spouse. They are:

1. To sell the asset you must have your joint tenant's cooperation and participation. For example, if you are selling your house and your son is a joint tenant, he and his wife must also "sign off" before you will be able to complete the sale.

2. The asset is vulnerable to your joint tenant's divorce, lawsuits and creditors. For example, if your daughter is a joint tenant on your bank account and she is sued, her creditors can collect from your bank account.

3. Will

If your assets pass to your spouse, children, family member or friend by Will, THE ASSETS MUST FIRST GO THROUGH PROBATE. The preceding sentence may surprise you as most people believe that if they have a Will, they have avoided Probate. Not true. If assets pass by Will, they must go through Probate.

Why so? Because at your death if there are assets in your name alone, only a Probate Court can transfer those assets to the persons named in your Will.

The purpose of a Will is to tell the Probate Court who is to receive your estate, who is to administer your estate (the personal representative or executor) and who is to be guardians of minor children.

4. No Will

If at your death there are assets in your name alone and you do not have a Will, your assets must still pass through Probate. And the laws of your state will dictate who will receive the assets.

5. Living Trust

A Living Trust is similar to a Will because it says who is to receive your assets at your death (and the death of your spouse if you are married) and who is to administer the Trust (the trustee).

You create a Living Trust by signing a legal document called a Trust Agreement. You (and your spouse) are the trust maker, the trustee and the beneficiary. If you and your spouse each have your own trust, you and your spouse will be the trustees of both trusts and the beneficiaries of both trusts. You can change or revoke your trust at any time.

As the trustee and the beneficiary, you manage the trust and you have full use of the trust assets during your lifetime. If you become incapacitated and at your death, the person you have named as your successor trustee takes over.

A living trust is especially useful if your become disabled or incapacitated because your successor trustee is authorized to take over the management of the trust assets. If a successor trustee does take over because of your illness or incapacity, the trust assets are used *exclusively* for your support and care (and that of your spouse.)

Trust Terms

A Living Trust is created while you are alive. A Testamentary Trust is created at your death through your Will. A Revocable Trust can be changed or revoked at any time during your lifetime. An Irrevocable Trust cannot be changed or revoked. A revocable trust becomes irrevocable at your death. A Revocable Living Trust is created while you are alive and can be changed or revoked until your death.

Children with Special Needs

If you have a child with "special needs" who receives or may receive government benefits, an inheritance may make the child ineligible for the benefits. A Living Trust with *specific special needs provisions* will safeguard the child's current and/or future benefits.

Selecting a Trustee

The trustee will be the person responsible for managing and distributing your child's inheritance. Therefore he or she should have successful financial experience, share your views about money and be young enough to survive until your youngest child reaches the age you've specified for his or her final distribution.

The guardian and trustee may be the same person but they don't have to be; the decision is yours. If the guardian and trustee are not the same person, keep in mind that they will have to peacefully co-exist for the benefit of your children for what could be a long time.

Age is also a factor. While grandparents may be the best choice today, as they get older they may no longer be the best choice.

If your trust is to continue after your children turn 18, the guardian will be out of the picture but the Trustee will continue until your youngest child reaches the age you've specified in the Trust.

Always, Always Name Backup Guardians and Trustees

I strongly recommend that you name backups for both the guardian and trustee. Better still, review and revise (if necessary) your estate plan regularly. If you've named grandparents as guardian and/or trustee and that's no longer in your children's best interests, revise your estate plan documents. Revisions are usually not expensive because you are amending your existing documents rather than starting from scratch.

Other Reasons for Using a Living Trust

Trusts are used for reasons other than protecting the finances of minor children. Trusts are also used to safeguard governmental benefits that are or may be received by disabled children or adults. And trusts if properly funded avoid probate.

A Trust CAN Avoid Probate

When you (and your spouse) are deceased, your successor trustee distributes the assets to the person or persons you've named as the beneficiaries of your trust. **If** your assets are in the name of your Trust, the assets will pass directly to the trust beneficiaries thereby avoiding Probate. However, if your assets are not in the name of your Trust, the assets must first go through Probate to get to your trust beneficiaries.

As discussed in Chapter 4, your Attorney will transfer your assets to your trust by changing the title of the asset from your name (and your Spouse's name if he or she is also on the title) into the name of your Trust.

The primary difference between a will and a trust is a trust can avoid Probate. A will cannot avoid Probate.

Other Reasons to Use a Living Trust

Trusts are used for reasons other than to avoid Probate, for example: If you're in a marriage that blends children from prior relationships, a trust or trusts can provide for the children of both spouses regardless of the sequence of deaths. Trusts are also used to protect distributions to minor children and to safeguard governmental benefits that are or may be received by disabled children and/or adults.

Estate Planning for a Blended Family Can be Contentious!

Estate Planning for a married couple with a blended family can be a source of conflict for the married couple, their children and even the attorney. You and your spouse may not see eye to eye about who gets what at the first death and again at the second death. This area of estate planning is so complex that you must employ an experienced estate planning attorney. And you may end up employing two attorneys because of the potential conflict of interest between spouses.

If you have minor children you will also need to name guardians for them. Please review the Chapter "Estate Planning With Minor Children."

Options for Blended Families

- Divide the assets between the spouses and then each spouse takes care of his or her own children; or

- Take care of your spouse, but make sure your own children eventually get your assets; or

- Both spouses provide for their respective children, each other and their children from the current marriage; or

- Leave everything outright to your spouse and then the children of both spouses.

Issues to Consider

- Do both spouses want to transfer their wealth to their children from their first marriage?

- Are there family heirlooms and/or a family business to protect?

- Are both spouses financially independent?

- Will "death taxes" complicate the distribution at the death of the first spouse?

- Will a plan that reduces death taxes also reduce the surviving spouse's control of the money?

- What about the marital residence and the furniture and furnishings; who gets them?

- Will the surviving spouse be able to maintain his or her current standard of living at the death of the first spouse?

-Will the children of the first spouse to die receive "their share" at the death of their parent? Or will they have to wait until the death of their step-parent?

- If the surviving spouse lives for a long time after the death of the first spouse, will the distributions to the children be delayed until the surviving spouse dies? If so, the surviving spouse may not like the idea that stepchildren are eagerly awaiting his or her death to receive their inheritance.

NINE

OTHER POSSIBLE ESTATE PLANNING ISSUES

If You Have a Companion Pet or Pets, Do You Want to Include Them in Your Estate Plan?

In most states pets are considered personal property rather than individuals with rights. Consequently your pet or pets will pass to your legal heirs unless you have made other legal arrangements. There are three types of legal documents that will safeguard your pet if you become disabled and at your death. If this is an objective of your estate plan, be sure to discuss this with the Attorney at the initial meeting.

If You Have Firearms, Do You Want to Include Them in Your Estate Plan?

Firearms are a unique type of personal property with separate rules and regulations that can affect your estate plan. If you have firearms, be sure to discuss them with your Attorney.

Get Started

"Knowledge is Power" but only if the knowledge prompts action. Get a recommendation for an experienced estate planning attorney. Make an appointment. Take your Checklists to the appointment and follow them. Your reward will be an Estate Plan that meets your needs and objectives and the peace of mind that comes from knowing that you have made things as easy as possible for your family at your disability or death.

About the Author

Julie A. Calligaro is the author of nine books including *A Guide For Widows And Widowers and Estate Planning In Plain English*. She is a Partner in the firm of Calligaro & Meyering P.C., an Estate and Gift Tax Lawyer of the Year, and former member of the Ethics Committee, Henry Ford Hospital and Riverside Hospital.